936730

D1353837

STEEPLECHASE PARK

AQUINAS
LEARNING RESOURCES
CENTRE

ACC No.	936730
CLASS No.	821914 NAG
DATE	13. 1. 1997

Frances Nagle

STEEPLECHASE PARK

Rockingham Press

Published by
The Rockingham Press
11 Musley Lane,
Ware, Herts
SG12 7EN

Copyright © Frances Nagle, 1996

British Library Cataloguing-in-Publication Data

A catalogue record for this book
is available from the British Library

ISBN 1 873468 45 8

Printed in Great Britain
by Bemrose Shafron (Printers) Ltd,
Chester

Printed on Recycled Paper

*For Will and Liz
and my friends*

Acknowledgements

Acknowledgements are due to the editors of the following publications in which some of these poems first appeared: *As Girls Could Boast* (Oscars Press), *Envoi, Five Women Poets* (Crocus), *Lancaster Literature Festival Anthology (1994)*, *London Magazine, Poetry Nottingham, The North, Orbis, Poems from the Readaround* (Tarantula), *The Rialto, Risk Behaviour* (Smith/Doorstep), *Stand Magazine, Staple* and *Windfall* (Kettleshill Press). Acknowledgements are also due to the BBC Radio Network North West. 'War Baby' was the winning poem in the 1994 Southport Writers' Circle Open Competition. Some of the poems in this collection first appeared in the pamphlet *Visit to the Illuminator* (Dagger Press, 1994). I would like to thank North West Arts Board for a writer's bursary awarded to me in 1993.

Contents

Flotilla

Small comfort in the company when each one knows
He sails his skiff alone.
The harbour mouth will call me once too often
— Soft and gentle is the deep at nightfall —
Riffling breezes tease my oil-lamp; as it peters out
I look across:
Your glow persisting is my consolation.
It will be logged:
The vessel went down contesting on a great sea.

Lute Music

for Roger Child

You play your lute
As if I am not here; as if
What you do together
Is intimate.

Though the air sounds,
It is incidental, surely,
To this act where give and take
Combine.

Music happens
Like this rarely:
Eden — its appalling brevity —
Sung.

Play your lute
Like this:
As if I am not here;
As if you are not.

Prelude, Galliard,
Riserectione:
Pluck them once only.
Once, only.

No Music for the Wedding

No music in his church in Lent —
The priest was adamant.
But what was music?

Once, it had been Mozart's
Clarinet Concerto — the adagio —
Over and over: love

Rendered for the first time;
Its enunciation;
Closing bar.

She must have made her progress
Down the aisle in silence:
She does not remember.

Nor the sob
Of the clarinet
Outside the church.

Epithalamion

Suppose that we unswear our oath;
Untie this knot that binds
Our enemy to us;

Unstitch the white, white dress
From which my body nightly
Soars beside its mortalness;

Untake our photographs;
Unbear our fruit; untwine our stems;
Neuter the oestrus that began

My cursed campaign.
Unbuild the folly that was love
Where no love proved. This done,

Suppose that when we join
In pleasure our capricious flesh,
The enemy is gone.

Picture: House on the Moor

It does not deceive us for a moment.
Though you hang it in our bedroom,
You know as well as I do
What we do not say:

That the house so bridally poised
In ivory silk impasto,
Attended by sea-green fells,
Cannot hold its pose;

That as the artist turned to go,
Black empty windows wearily closed;
Sandstone blocks sagged, uncoupled,
Tumbled the whole desolate valley down;

That smoke, apparently rising from the chimney,
Tells the least effective lie of all:
For this is a house that no fire can warm.

And yet you bring it home.

Gift

Here is my gift
Of words I cannot say;
All that is left
Of love's boundless chatter —
Its husk and its shadow.
Open it later.

Michal's Secret

*Therefore Michal the daughter of Saul had no child
unto the day of her death.*
                              Samuel 1.18—2.6

What my sisters do not understand
Is how my body, Phaltiel, remains with you
Even as I sleep in King David's bed
And act as he commands.

My sisters burn still for the lovely boy
Sent by God to show what God is like;
He who aroused desire in everyone.
My crazed father gave him, briefly, to me.

I have heard of a country where a virgin
As part of her betrothal lies with a stranger,
That the once-and-for-always loss of her treasure
May not blemish the love she will know with her husband.

Though, Phaltiel, I am reclaimed by the stranger,
Ours is the unblemished love.
The King will never seed a prince in Michal,
Not for all his godlike strength and power.

After Sodom

Once my sister had voiced the thought
There was no going back.
For the sake of our race, she said,
For the good of the tribe.
I saw him then, not as our father, Lot,
But as male; carnal.
I was ashamed.

When she took him drunk and senseless
Into her body, I looked away.
I called for our mother to melt
And be flesh again.
When she rose this morning
She wore a look of knowing.
It lies between us.

I have run from the cave
Where she busies herself like a wife,
Sponging his skin, preparing the wine
We will make him drink to excess.
I look down the hill
Onto cinders — our city, our people
Consumed by ungoverned greed.

I have no stomach for the task ahead.
And yet ... I have seen him that way now;
How would I ever forget?

The Wanderer

I

I dare not think of you, Calypso,
Your slow seduction of me every night,
Fire low-burning in the hearth,
Its scent of cedarwood and juniper.

Gentle gaoler
For seven years,
And not a day I did not weep
For Ithaca.

Now I am returned to those I loved —
My father, my son, my constant wife.
But she grows old:
Penelope is only mortal.

I dare not think of you
In your cavern, singing,
Weaving your golden shuttle
To and fro;

Or your magical island
Carpeted in irises,
Watered by crystal streams,
Where I take you, Calypso, in my dreams.

II

She screwed his letter up
And, as she tried to smooth it out again,
Repeated — many times — his name:
O d y s s e u s.

16

Her answer could bring him
Scudding across the bay.
He would find her ready and
He would not say no.

Nor would he say *Penelope is history* —
And stay.

III

We have not met. If we had
I would have guessed,
For if you were even half human
Your avoiding eyes would have given you away.

But I know you exist:
My husband's spirit flails against
The spell you have woven round him;
He has lost himself.

I beg you, one woman to another,
Meet me face to face.
Let me look upon your power,
See what my enemy is.

Or else in secret, by moonlight,
Unweave the shroud my Odysseus wears.
It can be done;
I know it.

Telethusa's Daughter

after Ovid

Ignis is a man of tender feeling;
His love for me has been beyond all praise.
When he told me we would put to death a girl-child
We wept as one stricken parent.

To understand how your father could do this
You have to know what it is to be free-born
But poor, and the spectre of slavery
Only a slim dowry away.

I prayed to be delivered of a son.
It was not to be.
But the night before you were born
Io appeared to me in dream.

She stood at the foot of the bed
And told me there was a way:
To pretend that my child was a boy.
The gods smiled on my deceit.

Iphis you have been the perfect daughter,
The perfect son.
You trusted in your mother,
Obeyed your father,

Acquiesced to the marriage he contracted,
Even fell in love with the chosen bride.
All day I weep and pray for you,
Torn apart by love for your own kind.

I hear you cry that you wish you had not lived.
I put off the wedding-date time after time.
We haunt Io's temple and howl — *Io,*
Have pity on us.

Today the doors of the temple trembled,
Her altars moved across the tiles,
Her horns gleamed like the horns of the moon,
Her piercing rattle shrilled.

Now as we walk back home
I sense that your stride is longer,
Your face has a coarseness about it,
Your voice has deepened.

What kind of loss is this
That a mother has to suffer
To give her child life?
Farewell, daughter.

I, Gruoch

I, Gruoch, come to you, Macbeth,
To be your Lady. Slim recompense
For your father's slaughter
At my husband's hands.

Gillacomean was brutal;
Those who say I have too soon
Warmed your bed
Have never lain with him.

Hush my Lord — the sound of his name
Inflames you. Gillacomean
Was such a fool to say
This lion does not roar.

When he murdered your father
He scoffed at the thought
That you might render
His child orphan.

My Lord, stroke me
There — and there. Who would think
To find such sweetness
In so bold a warrior?

They who burned alive the husband
Should have burned the son;
Lulach the Simple is not fit to be
My heir.

Kiss me — let us begin
To lay down our lineage.
Such sons you and I will breed, Macbeth!
History will honour us for this.

An Heir for Bonaparte

1808

One afternoon in July, I visited the Empress
At Malmaison. We walked in her gardens, rested
Under the glass dome of her palm house.
She shivered.

Again and again I told her what was true —
That I had heard nothing at court that might alarm her.
As far as I knew the Emperor had never uttered
The word Divorce.

She told me I could not imagine the envy
That coursed through her veins, the poison.
And indeed I could not, for she had always been
Most tender-hearted.

She gathered my little daughter in her arms.
"Tell me, Madame Junot, how do I bear it?
To see a woman like you with your beautiful child:
The joy of its mother, but above all

The hope of its father?"

1810

Imperial pressures:
No one can understand
Who hasn't woken daily
To the crush of them.

My love, my Josephine,
My own true wife.
What would I not have given
For a child with her?

But the state demands.
Tomorrow we marry Austria
And, by the grace of God,
She will conceive.

Though our triumphal arch
Is not yet built,
I have had Chalgrin raise on its site
A mock façade.

The new Empress
On her nuptial ride,
Will see how great
A dynasty this is.

This Sunday

This Sunday after church we decide, on the spur
                  of the moment, to visit my sister.
Strange how the pain of it can grab when you least expect it —
A glass of wine too many, I sit in a garden chair and watch
                          my brother-in-law
Teach his son to play cricket. Both of them so earnest.

I mention it to my wife on the journey home.
                      "For months," she says,
"You kid yourself the wound is healing.
                  It's ten-and-a-half years since
Our final *in vitro*. Yet still, sometimes, I catch myself
                       waking exultant
Out of a dream in which it's been successful."

How she can do her job, I just don't know.
                    Surrounded by them.
"It doesn't bother me there," she says, "or hardly ever.
It's when I'm relaxed, when my mind's free-wheeling."
In my sister's garden it had struck her.
                Like news of a death —

The loss of our grandchildren.

The Bull and I

for Vicki Moore

After they'd lured you away from what was left of my body,
They had you shot.
So reluctant you'd been to go; knowing by now
That you could not trust those silky voices —
We won't hurt you.

I lay in my hospital bed, all pain.
Surfacing out of the coma, I longed for death,
Its anaesthesia.

Every time I closed my eyes for the mercy of sleep
You charged me again, your horns ripped in.
Again and again you scooped out my flesh.
You skewered my lung.

I wanted to cry out *Argentino, you've got it wrong —*
I want to save you.
But you are insane now, goaded to frenzy
By darts from the crowd.   A banderillo
Is hooked deep in your shoulder, through
Your hide, into the meat below.
You smell your own blood.

Your horns stab into my body. In.   In.

* * *

This evening my terror is gone.
You, my gentle visitant, stand by the bed.
As if to say *We have been to the same place.*

Now we are brothers under the skin.
As if to say you are sorry, you misunderstood —
I cannot be blamed for being
Of the human race.

I have never seen eyes so full of trust;
They beg me not to forget.
Tonight, at last, I will sleep in peace.
When I am well I'll film the bulls again.

Three Sorrows

Can you imagine what they carve away
From little girls? What it costs
To bear the mark of an African woman?
Why we must walk so proud?

Let me show you my mark, my pride.
Look. Here, on my wedding night,
My husband's family slit me. It
Entered an open wound.

And here, the doctor slit again
To let my daughter out. He sealed
Me up so sadly, the European doctor:
Stitched the place as if he'd loved it.

Ukrainian Mother

In the end women got together
And refused to take their babies to the hospitals;
So many died there. Like Olga.

The order came for a check-up; routine.
They kept her, and wouldn't let me in.
One day they told me she had died.

They gave sweets to my other daughter,
Put Olga's death certificate before me,
Showed me where to sign.

Today I have been told I put my name
To a paper giving her away.
Rich Americans paid many dollars.

They say such crimes will not occur again.
Too late for me and the other mothers
Who lost our babies because we could not read.

A young woman doctor has been put in prison.
Not the officials who issued documents
With a speed unheard of in the Ukraine.

The Greatcoat

after a story by Gogol

Winter, that old assassin,
Is in the air.

The man with a worn-through greatcoat
Had hardly eaten for months

But has scraped sufficient roubles for a garment
To keep him this side of freezing.

He parts with them almost gaily, and for a moment
Fear is chased from his city.

Death follows the theft of his greatcoat as surely as ice
Clinches the Neva.

Perhaps, and this is not unlikely,
The thief was another who had nothing.

Even so.

Leaving the Artist

I wish I'd never set eyes on you.
I'm trying to gather my things —
My jars, my wicker chair, my canvases;
Trying to get myself together.

You have me hanging everywhere.
All my eyes follow me, unzip
My clothes, and further,
Watch me decompose.

The stone you sent for has arrived.
I shall not stay to see myself
Emerge; to hear my excess
Clink upon the tiles.

I tried to leave you once before.
You often tell it; how you were
Deranged. But I remember
How I sagged back in

And you were urgent, urgent, and
Must show me how the sky was brushed
With violet, rose. If you were here
I could not tell you this.

An Artist Paints Her Life

Sometimes after such encounters
All she could remember
Was a ceiling and a lightshade.

Suddenly nights later
She must paint a pleated circle
On a crazed white oblong
And would get that feeling
In her chest — a lung exploding —
While her mind's eye saw a picture:
Sky as blue as California,
Poppy-orange sun.

Then she'd run down to the city,
Trawl its bars,
For the next mark on her canvas.

Je m'amuse

Perhaps now I can see
Why Robert Graves drew
Down so many women;
What impelled him.

Why he laid them
Body and soul
Against him
On white sheets.

How in all honesty
He could blame his Goddess.
How the penis hardly
Entered into it.

As I steal on men
And write them into love poems;
Lie in impossible conjunctions;
Perhaps I see.

Visit to the Illuminator

The normal eye is out of phase.
So spare the gesture of her nib
We do not see it move, though move
It must, as flowers must unfold.

Our chase is cornered in this room
Where calm is ruling. We begin
To listen for the catch of quill
On vellum; time unwinding.

How can this be so slow?
How can so little happen?
We have driven across centuries
To see a woman doing almost nothing.

Machines can humble every skill
She demonstrates: line, colour,
Pattern, snaking curlicue. "Why does
She bother?" someone whispers.

She does not answer him with speech.
The hand that hardly stirs
Embellishes beyond his sight
A word.

We move off to another place
Of interest — fast on the heels
Of rumour: truth, inevitably,
Taking longer.

The Other Woman

SUMMER

In August he sends
A postcard from Gascony
Or somewhere: unblemished
Beach; sky; ocean;
One figure
Scanning the horizon.

She feels the hot sand
Melt beneath her toes.
She tastes salt spray.
And sees — just out of
Sight — two deckchairs
Turned away.

BONFIRE NIGHT

Display is in the air.
In a park that's close
(But not too close) to
Home, they hold hands,
Kiss, and watch last
Season's wood turn
Crackling gold.

The night is moved
To shower them with
Rockets, fountains.
Children sparkle
The sky with words —
As she does:
His name, her name.

CHRISTMAS DAY

He will not call.
His children have arrived
With young, staking
Their annual claim
To birthright; driven
To honour breeding grounds
They take for granted.

She plays three-handed bridge
All afternoon; a bastard
Variant of the game in which
Her parents, suffering infirmity,
Sit tight, and she moves over
East to West to East;
Is always dummy.

HER BIRTHDAY

Dressed-up in hope
She waits: remembers
Her first birthday
When he skipped work
To drive her to the sea.
He gave her the whole day
And the night.

Not the year he bought
His wife the same fragrance.
Or the year he forgot.
She watches through
Her window; plays
Game upon game
Of patience.

* * *

In August he sends her a postcard
From Gascony or somewhere.

Close Reading

I write, reluctantly,
To say I must put off
The visit I intended.
We intended.

Events require my presence —
People need me — I should
Remain here.
You'll understand.

But if you did
You'd write again, post haste —
Come now, at once,
I want you — you would say.

And nothing would keep me away.

Monody

Summer spell:
And we, who would have
Passed each other,
Caught.

Can you recall
That feeling — lost
Before we found it —
Enchantment round us

Letting go?
Its ends
Like my hands falling
From your waist.

Amphibian Love-Song

We hear you more than a mile away
Revving up your stretched-elastic song,
A thousand voices with the timbre
Of a rubbed balloon.
Above them all I hear my darling,
My own handsome spadefoot, garlic-scented,
Buzzing with lust, chest puffed proud,
In this day's new-minted pool
In the broiling desert of Arizona,
Beneath a smiling moon.

I will shovel free from my cool coffin
To swarm with the urgent, ripe females
Who converge now on your maleness
Like an imploding star. And there
You are — the water thrutching with expectation.
You find me.
And as your foreleg slips around my waist,
My eggs slither down.
Tomorrow we will feed and part.
All year I will listen for your call.

Looking for Heathcliff

Today the moor was drenched in cloud,
My gown weighed heavy.
All I could see was wind-scoured
Rock and heather. I searched
For the tracks of his horse,
Felt at the back of caves
For empty wine-skins.

Tonight by the parlour fire
My sister is attentive to the curate,
Who stuffs his smooth pink cheeks
With seed-cake as he chatters.
His fish eyes gleam,
But not, I fear, for my sister
Who has told me that she thinks
That she may love him.

On the moor —
He's riding.
The wind that rocks our chimney
Rushes through his hair.
If I draw aside the curtain
I will see how the cloud has lifted;
How under a great white moon
He gallops across the skyline
On his bold black mare —
His body
Close upon her withers
As she beats against the tempest.

Steeplechase Park

after a painting by Reginald Marsh

In Steeplechase Park
We ride and we swing,
We light up in the dark,
We forget all our pain
In the lift and the flight:
Everything's thrilling,
Everything's right.

We roll onto our backs,
Our skirts billow high,
Our legs open slightly,
There's a look in our eye
Alluring the riders
Who smile at us hard
Before they divide us.

In Steeplechase Park
A man tries to mount
The mare of his choice
And finds that he can't.
He wallops her rump,
Then has her shot,
Says the filly won't jump.

The Composer Amy Beach

Phenomenally gifted as a child, she soon acquired a reputation as a piano virtuoso, but this was later superseded by a recognition of her accomplishments as a composer. She was the first composer in America to write a symphony of importance.

PERCY A. SCHOLES:
The Oxford Companion to Music

I

Amy, we must put a stop to this.
What is it Calvin tells us? *Take from a child*
That thing he loves most.
Since you could toddle you've played
Every song we've sung you.
We do this for your own dear sake.

II

We could never make out how Mrs. Cheney
Could be that cruel. But, in any case,
There was no stopping the child.
Without her piano she took to playing
The stairs — knelt on the bottom one,
Played her tunes on the next.
Stood her music on the one above.
She was always to be found there; always.
One day a visitor called and had words
With Mrs. Cheney. We didn't hear
What was said, but from that day on
Amy played piano all the time.

III

I have been the most fortunate of women,
With loving parents, my fine husband, my music.
They said that when I was small I mastered Chopin
Even though my hands were the hands of an infant.
But somehow, according to Mother, I knew
Which of the notes it was best to leave unplayed.
My concerts made Boston the focus of the world.
I adored making music; I was adored.
In the contract I signed on my marriage to Doctor Beach
Was a clause that said I would cease to play in public.
Young women ask me how did that feel?
I don't remember. They find it hard to believe.
But I thank God daily for it now;
For guiding me down this road.

Purveyors

"Yes sir. We'll get you any title.
The Joy of Evil. Do you know the author?
Dawn of Darkness. No, we don't deliver."
Please don't look into my eyes like that, sir.

The house is not dissimilar to mine:
Two bedrooms, boxroom, cosy street.
His voice is velvet unction; his pants are tight.
I deliver — night after night after night.

Lover

If I look
From my bedroom
I can almost see your house;

Your children —
Count them through their birthdays;
Setting out;

Your wife,
A naked blur
Behind the bathroom window;

And you,
Across the bed,
Or putting your clothes on briskly,

Your watch,
Her present,
Snapping against your skin.

Lady-in-Waiting

The King was here tonight:
He brought me emeralds.
This collar and this brooch.
He stayed until the flames
That licked the applewood
Had died. I lie here
Warm of his royal breath.

The King was here tonight.
We dined on pheasant —
I had spent the day
Preparing it. He sighed
And said it was the finest
Ever. He gazed at me
As if he were my subject.

I didn't think of the Queen.
Or if I did she belonged
To a different story. The one
In which I was a pure spinster;
Or a name hissed behind hands
In polite circles.
I try not to think of her.

As he made his progress
Through my assenting body,
As he took deep charge,
My soul whirled bewildered
Then knelt to pay him homage.
In applewood dreams he takes me,
And promises a kingdom.

Something Aunt Rosie Said

"Our lads never got a look-in
After the Yanks came. You
Were nearly a G.I. baby
In my opinion, but never tell
Your mother I said so.

I remember, night after hot night,
Trying to listen from the window
While they cuddled in our shed,
And did things I couldn't make out
At the time: and some of their names —
Marty, Darren, Wayneford,
B. J. Stevenson the Third.

Our Mam, she said it was
The nylons, instruments of sin,
That those that give them
Think they have the right ...

I was too young for more
Than chewing-gum, but I
Could feel their — I dunno —
Their hugeness, all the space
That each one carried around him,
Colossal magnetic fields, charisma
We'd call it now, pzazz, you'll
Be okay with us babe,
The winning team.

Sometimes, afterwards, she'd
Whisper me from her bed
And tell me things.

Oh bliss, she'd say, it's all
Such bliss. I try to think
About them, Rosie, out there,
Our boys — and she'd fling her arm out
Showing me the sky — but Rosie, Rosie
It's all such fun, and Rosie
Darling, you've seen nothing
Till you've seen a Yankee soldier
Loading up his gun."

Miniature Portraits of Two Little Girls

after Isaac Oliver 1590

Observe, he says, this universe. He opens it.
They peep out — four years old; four hundred;
Tiny Tudors in stiff, white ruffs, heart-faced:
Mock ladies in black and golden silks
That rustle like court conspiracies.
Listen, he says, for their stifled shrieks
As they play to the rules of inheritance —
The game is adult; no one is innocent.

Are there always girls who examine us
As she on the left so grimly smiling does,
Her bloom of thrift inalienably squeezed:
Or she on the right so glumly acquiescent
That I laugh; would wrap her in my arms, ease
The apple out of her unwilling hand?

War Baby

1

It was as if he were the firstborn,
Coming as he did with perfect timing
Nine months after war ended.
He never looked back;
His slightest act delighted.
He had only to lift a spoon
For our father to say to Mother
"Would you credit that?"

She did what she could for us:
"See what Peter has made, what Winifred has written."
"Very good, very good," he'd say,
Or "Neater would have been better."
Or words never spoken:
Why aren't you more like your brother?

2

Home to a house that's colder than I remember;
To a woman who calls herself my wife
Who masquerades as the girl in my letters —
The one I betray her with each night.

The children cling to her dress and do not smile.
Their names won't fit the pictures in my head.
Perhaps that explains the loneliness I feel,
The loss of the closeness we shared when I was absent.

Come to me Peter, Winifred, call me Father.
Bring me your toys to mend, bring me your kite.
I will set it in the sky for you
To chase away the blankness in your eyes.

3.

All I wanted was the war to end,
And you — returned to me unharmed.

That day I understood what we had lost:
The children hid behind me; when we kissed

Peter screamed.
"He'll get used to you," I said.

In bed as you blindly rode
Over years of ruined land

I wished you a loving, laughing son;
Lay beneath you starting life again.

The Young Persons' Guide to the Second World War

after reading "Children at War", edited by
Patricia Williams

I

A night for love
In Europe, Asia,
Scandinavia;
A child is born
Somewhere, later.
Luck of the bedroom,
Luck of the draw.

II

Don't say they were lucky,
Jews like Maman,
Alone, unapparent
In Catholic families;
Jews who survived.
Yellow star
Fixed to the coat
That she wouldn't wear
Unless an emergency
— One of the children —
Forced her out on the street.

Living in dread
Of a knock on the door.
When it came
We tore up floorboards,
Nailed her in.

We read her telegram
On telegram. And sang.
Not all our singing
Could cover her howl.
She survived.
Not lucky at all.

III

*'Every Pole who survived the war has a horror
story to tell.'*

Jan Ciechanowski

I was ten.
I watched Germans
The age of my father
Drive a file of children,
Some of them only toddlers,
Into our woods.

I heard shots.
I watched the Germans
Return alone
Laughing, cracking jokes.
I watched them quench their thirst
With lemonade.

IV

From the moment the Germans came
They treated us with kindness.
I believe they would have liked
To let us go, except they knew
We would betray them.

They brought us food daily:
Black bread, ham, chocolate;
Permitted Papa to leave the cellar once
To collect some precious family possessions:
Toothbrushes, photographs, letters.

For ten minutes Rotterdam was bombed:
Twenty-four thousand houses down.
Our German soldiers sang to cover the sound,
That the small fair-haired Dutch girl
Wouldn't be frightened.

V

In Finland,
Russia's back door,
Nailed down to stop the enemy
From taking us off our hinges,
We knew perpetual hunger.

I can still taste it;
And molten tar
That we peeled from roads,
Almost as good
As chewing gum.

VI

Christmas in Lombardy:
Under the tree
A few simple toys,
Nuts, tangerines.

In the oven
Papa's resistance,
Two fat turkeys
Reared in secret.

A knock at the door:
Three German officers,
Others to follow.
We slip from the table.

In the kitchen
Our maid is stirring
Succulent gravy.
She beckons, and whispers.

My brother and I
Spit in the gravy,
Lick the turkey
All over.

VII

I look at the photographs now
And cannot tell you who are evacuees
And who are family.

They found us behind the times
And couldn't wait to get back
To the action in the city.

We found them rough and rude;
The boy who shared my bed
Wouldn't take his boots off.

They only ate out of tins
And were astounded to see cows in the fields
And milk appearing from them.

We thought their baked beans
The most wonderful food on earth.
These people were almost foreigners to us.

VIII

Once, an airman crashed into our wheat.
My father swung him onto his shoulders
Like a stillborn calf.

As he struggled back to life, he cried.
For his friends; for the linnet
That they'd taken up with them for luck.

IX

My brother the general
Took war seriously.
I was awarded the DSO
For displays of outstanding courage;
The DFC for my exploits in the air.
Hardest to win was the Victoria Cross,
Which he pinned to my chest
Posthumously.

X

I wanted to be in the navy
To be like my father.

I wore the same uniform
And felt very proud.

I longed for adventure
Like any boy my age;
And to be free of school,
Subjects I hated — History, Music.

My mother, like any woman,
Bought soap — nothing special
Just something to wash with —
On the black market.

My father, the good husband,
Did what they asked of him.
They released her.
She wasn't executed.

I was never a Nazi,
Nor were my parents.
I had nothing against Jews;
We didn't speak of them.

Defending the bridge
Began as a great adventure.
I was badly wounded
And received a medal.

I was sixteen when the war ended,
With one useless leg,
A fallen country.
Worse was to come.

XI

All the Hiroshima boys
Were eager to join the navy,
Spent hours down at the quay
Watching the warships return,
Saluting the sailors
In their uniforms of white
Trimmed with black braid.

My mother taught me
This was our holy war.
In school we were trained to kill;
I took up sport to refine
My body, my fighting machine.
I brought my family honour
In the sumo ring.

On a day we still remember,
Maybe in June, July,
My bout was over;
I watched my friend suffer
The shame of his loincloth
Working loose
And falling.

As he ran through the hall
Of screaming, laughing children
I can recall
How his hands, in vain,
Tried to protect his member;
And the flawless beauty
Of his skin.

Exhibit

Quite faultless:
Late twentieth century glass
Without bow or bubble.

Meat juices rusted it:
Their marks would rub away.
It could corral voices.

There are accounts from those who knew it —
It was impossible to see.
They used to walk right through it.

Country Dance

From above, they tell us,
We are one great loom
Of fluid lace;
Of breaking, coupling harmony.

Accordions gasp, fiddles thrill,
We circle, cross and cast.
Our hands suggest
And we avert our eyes.

They said of *Lusus Trojae* —
If you knew the dance,
You could tread the labyrinth
In the dark. Death's joke.

Breath dies inside accordions,
Fiddles lie cold.
We walk our lives through
Slipping hands.

Utopia

for Scott

We are learning about canals,
About their slow digging,
How their long straight stitches
Linked the slinky rivers
Into one great lacework.

You in your youthful wisdom
Say we should bring them back,
And horses to quietly haul
Down the watery lanes of England
The narrow way of living.

We close the history book,
It's time for Art — free choice.
You arrange your model,
A pink Viper Turbo,
The love of your life.

Hotel Anūgraha

We sit under this dome of glass
In a garden-room
Partitioned out of Surrey countryside.

A wedding, they have promised, like no other.
No formalities. No hats.
No hollow words. We sit in silence,
Strangely naked.

A girl starts singing *In My Life*
— A Beatles' number — beautifully.
I find I understand every word.

Here come the bride and groom.
Under the chupa they exchange
Old vows. Each syllable is measured:
The Lord, they say, is good.

I look around at Jews from England, Canada,
The Holy Land; recall a headline
In this morning's Independent:

Asians changing names to help job prospects.

A peacock butterfly has somehow found its way inside.
It folds its wings upon my neighbour's knee.

Filial

All day your arms lie at your side like fallen branches.
I search for answers in your fading face.
Was this a goddess, this her mighty fist?
I came as daughters come because they must.
I smooth your hair away maternally.
Where is the juggernaut?
Who is this easy, grateful lady?

I gather you to me.

Their Mothers

We three have never met
But there is always a place
Set for you at my feast-days.

One day you will arrive
Weary after long years of travel
Through the kind of hardship
That begins deceitfully small.

We will sit together
And tell our stories —
Of a land struck dead
By a curse; by a baby.

Of an ache — for something
So missing, that the sun
Turned its face to the wall
And earth turned to winter.

When it is time for your leaving
I will lend you a child
To light your journey home:

A son to defend you
From the forest phantoms;
A daughter with her
Dragon-soothing kisses.

The Verdict

There was no shortage of expert witnesses:
A diver declared that they were deep.
A bodybuilder was impressed by their strength.
A dentist pronounced them full of holes.
According to a doctor, they were getting better.
A psychiatrist was in two minds.
In the opinion of socialworkers
There was insufficient evidence of caring.
The police wanted to catch them and lock them up.
Politicians admired the ambiguities.

In the end though,
The only thing that counted,
Was the admission
By the man who drove for Pickfords
That he found them moving.

Paul Klee in Positano

*Later some Germans joined us at our table, but they were
refined people who didn't force their conversation on us.*

The Diaries of Paul Klee — April 3rd 1902

It might have been you and I
At the table in the Hotel de Roma,
The dining-room flooded with light.

If we had thought to look aside
From our anniversary meal,
We might have noticed him,

And his potential. And this meeting,
On the road between Sorrento and Amalfi,
Would have been the high moment of our lives.

He would, of course, have been mistaken
About our nationality; and the date,
For we were not yet born.

But he was right, we wouldn't
Have forced our conversation on him.
Even if we hadn't been so absorbed,

It is not in the British nature.
1902 was the year of my father's birth
In East Prussia.

Songs of Estrangement

1.   Folk-song

Back home there is a song
My blood would dance to
If I heard it.

Walls are built of years,
Of miles, I will not
Hear it now.

Sometimes a window opens slightly:
In the breeze I hear the wingbeat
Of a song I never used to know.

2.   The Wall Comes Down

Some who have made the journey
Say the air smells, not of ashes,
But of home;
That the sky is a colour
They have only seen in dreams;
That landscape closed its arms
Around each one.

I, who will not follow,
Will not meet my crate of dead
Upon their ground,
Am marked upon the map.

3.   *What Was Saved*

The tea-set
Alive with rose-blooms
That my mother handles
With priestly love.

Linen — embroidered by hand.

Silver knives and forks.
Their engraved letter H.

4.   *Reconciliation*

It is Lent.
I, a Moses-child,
Prepare to celebrate
The Passion of Our Lord.
And yet — the wind
That buffets from the east,
Across the land
That is for all time gone,
Breathes on me
With the hush of cradle-song.